Remembering
Fort Worth

Quentin McGown

TURNER
PUBLISHING COMPANY

The 1893 Al Hayne monument and fountain, lower right, no longer served as an oasis for thirsty horses and mules, whose jobs had been eliminated by automobiles and trucks by the time this photograph was taken around 1918. Within about ten years, the Texas & Pacific Railroad, owner of the magnificent passenger station built in 1900, would partner with the city of Fort Worth to redesign this intersection, replacing the old and dangerous grade crossings with a safer underpass at Main Street. The passenger station was replaced in 1929 by the Art Deco terminal still in use today.

Remembering
Fort Worth

Turner Publishing Company
www.turnerpublishing.com

Remembering Fort Worth

Copyright © 2010 Turner Publishing Company

Library of Congress Control Number: 2010924300

ISBN: 978-1-59652-646-4

Printed in the United States of America

ISBN: 978-1-68442-245-6 (pbk.)

CONTENTS

The Daggett and Hatcher store, at the corner of Houston and Weatherford streets, overlooks a bustling market scene about 1878. As cotton, produce, livestock, and other goods arrived in town to coincide with the sessions of the district court, proud Tarrant Countians posed for a photographer set up next to the courthouse.

ACKNOWLEDGMENTS

This volume, *Remembering Fort Worth,* is the result of the cooperation and efforts of a number of individuals.

Tom Wiederhold, Fort Worth Police Historical Association
Jim Noah
Jack White
Susan Pritchett, Tarrant County Archives
Donna Kruse, Tom Kellam, Jabari Jones and the staff of the Fort Worth Public Library Genealogy and Local History
Department
Louis Sherwood, Texas Wesleyan University Special Collections
Gilbert Anguiano
Pete Charlton, lectricbooks.com
Sarah Biles, North Fort Worth Historical Society
Beverly Washington
Sarah Walker
Brenda McClurkin, Ruth Callahan, and the staff of the University of Texas at Arlington Library, Special Collections
The staff at Turner Publishing
And, especially, my wife, Laurie, with deepest thanks.

—*Quentin McGown*

PREFACE

Fort Worth has thousands of historic photographs that reside in archives, both locally and nationally. This book began with the observation that, while those photographs are of great interest to many, they are not easily accessible. During a time when Fort Worth is looking ahead and evaluating its future course, many people are asking, How do we treat the past? These decisions affect every aspect of the city—architecture, public spaces, commerce, infrastructure—and these, in turn, affect the way that people live their lives. This book seeks to provide easy access to a valuable, objective look into the history of Fort Worth.

The power of photographs is that they are less subjective than words in their treatment of history. Although the photographer can make subjective decisions regarding subject matter and how to capture and present it, photographs seldom interpret the past to the extent textual histories can. For this reason, photography is uniquely positioned to offer an original, untainted look at the past, allowing the viewer to learn for himself what the world was like a century or more ago.

This project represents countless hours of review and research. The researchers and writer have reviewed thousands of photographs in numerous archives. We greatly appreciate the generous assistance of those listed in the acknowledgments of this work, without whom this project could not have been completed.

The goal in publishing this work is to provide broader access to this set of extraordinary photographs which seek to inspire, provide perspective, and evoke insight that might assist people who are responsible for determining Fort Worth's future. In addition, the book seeks to preserve the past with adequate respect and reverence.

With the exception of touching up imperfections that have accrued with the passage of time and cropping where necessary, no changes have been made. The focus and clarity of many images are limited to the technology and the ability of the photographer at the time they were recorded.

The work is divided into eras. Beginning with some of the earliest photographs of Fort Worth, the first section records photographs from the 1870s through the late nineteenth century. The second section spans the first decade of the twentieth century. Section Three carries the story forward to 1940. The last section covers the World War II era up to recent times.

In each of these sections we have made an effort to capture various aspects of life through our selection of photographs. People, commerce, transportation, infrastructure, religious institutions, and educational institutions have been included to provide a broad perspective.

We encourage readers to reflect as they go walking in Fort Worth, strolling through the city, its parks, and its neighborhoods. It is the publisher's hope that in utilizing this work, longtime residents will learn something new and that new residents will gain a perspective on where Fort Worth has been, so that each can contribute to its future.

—*Todd Bottorff, Publisher*

Looking east across the expansive public square from the intersection of Houston and Weatherford, this view shows the 1878 courthouse surrounded by a fence to keep stray animals out. The two-story building visible just to the right of the courthouse is the old Masonic Lodge, built in 1857, and used until 1878 for numerous community activities, including school and church sessions.

RAILROAD TOWN

(1870s–1899)

Hugh Dugan joined the flood of new residents in Fort Worth during the boom that followed the arrival of the Texas & Pacific Railroad in 1876. He started a laundry business about 1878 and expanded his property on Weatherford Street at Taylor to accommodate the transportation needs of the rapidly growing town.

David Boaz settled in Tarrant County with his family in 1859. He returned after his service in the Confederate Army and built a cotton brokerage business. He later partnered with George Battle to expand the business in the early 1880s to include buffalo hides and wool and to build a yard between Main and Houston from 13th to 14th streets, across from the railroad depot. A vertical sign on the utility pole appears to be an advertisement for Wizard Oil, a popular patent medicine.

Not long after the 1882 expansion of the courthouse, a photographer captured this view of the east side of the square and the growing city beyond. A new advertisement for Tippecanoe Bitters, a malaria "cure" patented in 1883, adorns a frame storefront typical of Fort Worth's early architecture. Next door stood the two-story Illinois Boarding House, successor to the Tarrant House. The blacksmith on the corner of what is now Commerce and Weatherford streets touted his services as "cheap and on short notice."

In 1893, German-born Sam Levy purchased this house on the southeast corner of Lamar and 7th streets from the heirs of John S. Hirshfield, whose 1874 addition to the city, with its grid aligned to true north, created the odd street angles in that section of downtown. Levy later served as president of the Casey-Swasey Cigar Company, one of the largest wholesale liquor and tobacco firms in the region. In 1903, he was a founder and the first president of Temple Beth-El, Fort Worth's first Reform Judaism congregation. He sold his home in 1919 to Bernie Anderson and Morris Berney, who erected the Neil P. Anderson building on the site.

In 1881, the Knights of Pythias, a charitable and fraternal organization chartered in Washington, D.C., in 1864 and established in Texas in 1872, built its first permanent lodge in Fort Worth at the corner of 3rd and Main. Damaged by fire in 1901, the building was rebuilt in Flemish style, complete with knight, and still presides over Main Street as the signature building in Sundance Square.

From its headquarters on lower Jones Street near the train depots, the Fort Worth Transfer Company delivered goods all over the growing town. E. A. Lewis, and other blacksmiths, kept the vehicles in good working order and occasionally worked on the draft animals as well.

The Eberhard Anheuser Company Brewing Association opened its first office in Fort Worth about 1878, a year before the firm changed its name to include Anheuser's son-in-law and partner, Adolphus Busch. The popular business quickly outgrew its small office and depot on Main Street and by 1885 expanded to the location shown here on the southeast corner of 3rd and Throckmorton streets. Delivery wagons kept local saloons and hotels supplied with the company's signature Budweiser beer. The company remained at this location until about 1892, when it left its German Gothic "castle" for larger facilities at Taylor and Front, now Lancaster Avenue.

On the night of May 30, 1890, fire broke out in the Texas Spring Palace building as more than 7,000 people enjoyed the fancy dress ball on the 16,000-square-foot dance floor. Miraculously, all but one escaped as the building was completely engulfed by flames in less than 15 minutes. Al Hayne stayed behind to direct people out of the burning building and was fatally injured when he finally was forced to jump from a second-story window.

Before its expansion and conversion into the Worth Hotel, the Hendricks Building was among the early "skyscrapers" in Fort Worth. Its five floors provided offices for some of the leading businesses in town. Soon after the building opened in the early 1890s, Pryor McDaniel greeted customers at his cigar store and newsstand at 807 Main.

The Texas Brewing Company's enormous plant on Jones Street (site of today's Intermodal Transportation Center) sent delivery wagons out across the city and kept businesses liberally supplied in Hell's Half Acre, near the present site of the Fort Worth Convention Center. The sprawling vice district covered much of the south end of downtown and was the chief source of problems for the city's lawmen.

In 1893, Tarrant County voters approved a $500,000 bond package to build a new courthouse to replace the outdated and outgrown 1878 courthouse. Designed along the lines of the 1888 State Capitol, and constructed of Texas pink granite, the building remains one of the most important structures in Fort Worth and is considered one of the finest of Texas' historic courthouses.

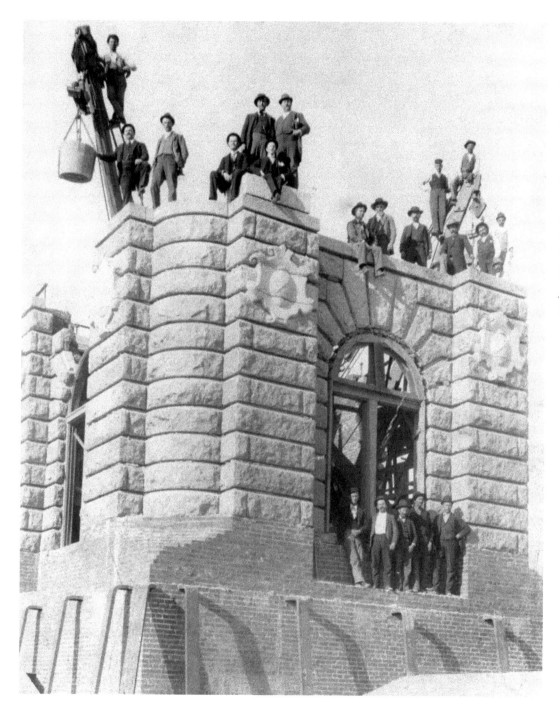

Construction foremen and proud county leaders braved the climb to the top of the courthouse during construction. At top, and standing third from left, is L. D. Nichols, granite foreman. Joining him are members of the commissioners court. Local lore says citizens outraged at the size and expense of the building voted all of them out of office the following year, even though it came in under budget. County Judge Robert G. Johnson sits on the ledge over the window right of center.

In 1896, a year after completion of the Tarrant County Courthouse, the federal government opened a new Post Office and Court building at Jennings and 11th to house the United States District Court of the just-created Fort Worth Division of the Northern District of Texas. Postal operations headquartered in the building oversaw mail service throughout Texas, Arkansas, Oklahoma, and Louisiana. In 1898, the U.S. Weather Bureau set its collecting instruments on the roof.

This image, recorded in December 1896, looks north on Jennings, past the just-opened red sandstone Federal Building and the 1893 Fort Worth City Hall beyond. Of all the buildings shown here, only the 1888 St. Patrick Cathedral, at right, remains standing today.

In order to stock his store at 7th and Burnett, Louis Bicocchi would ride out early to meet farmers as they came into town to sell at the market. Selecting the best produce to complement his wide selection of imported goods, he became one of the city's leading early grocers, catering to the wealthy families building their homes along Lamar and Burnett streets during the 1880s. Bicocchi later partnered with J. B. Laneri to found Fort Worth Macaroni Company in 1899. His store, shown here in 1894, was the first in town with electric lights and a cash register.

Fort Worth authorized its first police force shortly after the city incorporated in 1873, but financial constraints forced the small department to disband within a month. Before becoming a permanent city department in 1887, the police operated for a few years under the direction of town marshals, including, from 1876 to 1879, Jim Courtright, who would later die in a famous gunfight with gambler Luke Short. Here, several members of the force, including legendary officer George Craig, seated at left, pose in their summer (gray) and winter (blue) uniforms about 1895 in front of city hall at Throckmorton and 10th.

Fort Worth's love affair with baseball began in the 1870s, and blossomed after the 1887 creation of a Texas League comprising cities from across the state. The local team took its name from the town's famous mascot, the panther. This picture was taken in 1895, the year the team won its first championship. The Panthers would eventually shorten their name to the "Cats" and reach legendary status in the 1920s and 1940s. They played their final games in 1964. A new Fort Worth Cats minor league team revived the memories of its famous predecessors and began play at a rebuilt LaGrave Field in 2002.

Higher education expanded in Fort Worth in 1881 when the Methodist Episcopal Church opened Texas Wesleyan College. Outgrowing its original downtown facilities, the institution relocated in 1886 to a new site just outside the city limits, initially erecting four buildings, including University Hall, shown here. Green B. Trimble Technical High School occupies the College Avenue site of the old college, which was renamed Fort Worth University in 1889 and grew to include both law and medical schools before closing its doors in 1910. Texas Wesleyan College was not associated with today's Texas Wesleyan University.

The city's first "skyscraper" was the seven-story Hurley Building on the northwest corner of 7th and Main. Construction began in 1889 by the Fort Worth Loan and Construction Company, the firm chartered to build the Texas Spring Palace. Company president George L. Hurley helped transform the intersection of 7th and Main into the financial center of the city by leasing the ground floor to the newly established Farmers and Mechanics Bank, a location the bank would maintain until its acquisition by the Fort Worth National Bank in 1927.

This simple brick building on the northeast corner of 7th and Houston streets was home to Lee Whitsitt's Drug Store about 1898. A sign on the utility pole invites people to wait for the streetcar inside at the soda stand. In 1900, the First National Bank bought the lot and replaced the drugstore with an imposing two-story structure. That building was demolished in 1910 to make way for the bank's new home, a skyscraper designed by the city's leading architectural firm of Sanguinet and Staats. The bank building was restored in 2006 by XTO Energy and renamed for company chairman and CEO Bob R. Simpson.

Fort Worth welcomed spring with garden parties, dances, and parades. During the city's version of New York's Easter Parade, carriages and passengers were decorated in their finest. Here, a group of young women proudly pose for the camera. The street might be Belknap or Weatherford, once the heart of a fine residential neighborhood around 1900.

New Industry for a New Century

(1900–1910)

As Fort Worth grew to the south, following the arrival of the Texas & Pacific Railroad in 1876, new businesses followed. D. Mazza opened the first grocery store south of the railroad tracks. By 1900 the business, located at Jennings and West Daggett, was successful enough for the Mazza family to electrify their home around the corner from the store and become the first family on the south side to manage the Texas summer with the aid of an electric fan.

Adjacent to the streetcar barns was the three-story, brick, 1883 Tarrant County jail, designed by Houston architect Eugene Heiner. The image here shows the original street grading at Houston and Bluff streets for the first Main Street Bridge across the Trinity River, completed in 1890. Between billboards and salvage materials, the view greeting visitors coming into downtown from North Fort Worth seems less than inviting.

This scene from the intersection of Houston Street and 7th looking north about 1900 shows a growing and bustling city, with pedestrians dodging animals, manure, and streetcars to cross to the other side. The city's population at the time was about 25,000, but it would soon nearly triple as the economy boomed following the 1902 opening of the meat-packing operations in the Stockyards.

Main Street was equally busy as seen in this view north from 8th. The College Avenue streetcar heads south to Fort Worth University and the growing Fairmount neighborhood beyond. Behind the car is the 1890-era Wheat Building, whose limestone foundations, as well as portions of its former basement, are visible to visitors to the modern building on the site. In the next block stands the new, curved-front, 1899 Hoxie Building that replaced the burned Hurley Building.

The photographer's view from the front platform of a northbound streetcar captured a frequent frustration for the line's drivers—a buggy pulling out in front. Accidents were frequent, and the streetcars usually won. Ahead and to the left is the tower of the Commercial Club Building at 6th and Main. The Club, founded in 1885 and renamed the Fort Worth Club in 1909, demolished the building in 1915 to construct a new facility that would house the organization until 1926 when it moved to its new home at 7th and Throckmorton.

The courthouse dominated the city's skyline as the twentieth century began. The French Renaissance Revival masterpiece, designed by the St. Louis firm of Gunn & Curtiss, is considered by many as the most impressive county courthouse in Texas. In the lower center of this image, the cornice of the building at 1st and Main reads "Tidball, Van Zandt and Company, Bankers." Established in 1873, the private banking operation became the Fort Worth National Bank in 1884. Major K. M. Van Zandt served as president from 1874 until his death in 1930 at age 93.

A determined group of Fort Worth women established the Fort Worth Public Library Association in 1892. Struggling to raise funds through the lean years after the Panic of 1893, the group, led by Jennie Scheuber and Delphine Keeler, launched a campaign asking local men to donate the price of a good cigar. Sending the same solicitation to philanthropist Andrew Carnegie, Mrs. Keeler was rewarded with a $50,000 gift. The leveling of the cornerstone took place on October 17, 1901, attended by masons, musicians, and the beaming members of the Association.

Wagons and teams gather for a parade in front of the old Tarrant County jail on Belknap Street around the turn of the century. Seated at left in the buggy at the head of the line is John A. Mugg, Jr., partner in the ice, coal, and wood supply business of Mugg and Dryden, so artfully advertised on the sign held by his seatmate. Mugg came by his mercantile abilities naturally, being the grandson of Archibald Leonard who, with partner Henry Daggett in 1849, opened the first civilian store to serve the soldiers and settlers of Fort Worth.

North Fort Worth High School was renamed North Side High School in 1909, the year Fort Worth annexed the City of North Fort Worth. With no athletic program at the school, senior Wenzel "Runt" Stangel, center with ball, put a football team together and played the second teams of Central High School, Fort Worth University, and Polytechnic College, launching a school tradition of great football and legendary players. Stangel persuaded all of his teammates shown here to join him on the new baseball team the next year.

In 1910, the Flatiron Building still ranked among the city's tallest. Built in 1907 by Dr. Bacon Saunders, Dean of the Fort Worth University Medical School, the unique structure allowed local architects Sanguinet and Staats to bring a touch of New York and Chicago to Texas. Carved panther heads around the frieze memorialize the 1873 legend of a panther sleeping undisturbed on Main Street during an economic depression, the source of Fort Worth's nickname, "Panther City."

The Flatiron is at far-right in this bird's-eye view taken about 1910 from the roof of the Federal Building at Jennings and 11th streets. In the foreground at left is the 1893 Fort Worth City Hall, with the Tarrant County Courthouse looming behind it on the horizon. To the right of the city hall clock tower is the new First National Bank, designed by Sanguinet and Staats, and reigning, for a brief four-year period, as the tallest building in the city.

One of the more popular places in town at the turn of the century was the Sons of Hermann Park and Beer Garden located just across the river from the courthouse at the foot of the Main Street viaduct. Summer dances at the open air pavilion were a highlight of the season, although events were scheduled year round. Here, members and guests of the German Verein gather at the park for an evening's entertainment. Damaged during the Flood of 1908, the park site was selected for the location of a new North Main electric generating plant built by Fort Worth Power and Light in 1912.

Two buildings opposite each other on Houston Street at 8th represented the influence on the city of the cattle industry and the families who made their fortunes in it. The ornate, columned building at left was home to the Waggoner Bank and Trust, established in 1901 by W. T. Waggoner, owner of one of the largest ranching operations in the history of the United States. At right is one of the Reynolds Buildings, owned by G. T. and W. D. Reynolds, founders of the legendary Reynolds Cattle Company. One block away on the left in this image taken about 1905 is the 1889 Board of Trade Building.

Main Street looking north from the tower of the Texas & Pacific Station around 1904. Virtually every structure along Main, from the 1886 McCord Collins Building at lower-right to the Wheat Building at 8th Street, seen just left of the courthouse, was demolished for the Convention Center and Water Gardens. In the top left corner are St Patrick's Cathedral and the tower of the 1893 city hall at 10th and Throckmorton.

Captain M. B. Loyd, a Confederate veteran and native of Kentucky, arrived in Fort Worth in 1870, establishing an exchange office and becoming the city's first banker. In 1877, he received the ninth national bank charter issued in Texas and founded the First National Bank of Fort Worth, serving as its president until his death in 1912. Seated second from left, Captain Loyd poses here with officers and employees of the bank about 1900.

The T&P terminal burned in December 1904, drawing spectators from all over the city, including an enterprising photographer who climbed a telephone pole (far right) to capture the perfect shot. The station was rebuilt and used until it was replaced in 1929 by the modern Art Deco terminal still in use today. The left center of the photograph shows the monument and horse fountain dedicated in 1893 to the memory of Al Hayne, the hero and lone casualty of the Spring Palace fire of 1890. The fountain still stands on Lancaster, the sole survivor of this scene.

President Roosevelt paraded through town accompanied by veterans and cheered by crowds lining the streets and viewing from rooftops. In fact, one roof collapsed under the weight of 50 people straining to see the procession. No one was hurt, and the president continued to his next official duty, planting a tree in front of the Carnegie Library. Roosevelt visited the city again in 1911, speaking to a crowd in the North Side Coliseum.

In 1902, Fort Worth bicycle shop owner H. E. Cromer brought the first automobile to the city. While early motorists were cursed, shot at, threatened with flying beer bottles, and generally accused of disturbing the natural order of things, cars were here to stay. By 1904, there were 15 of them in town, including a Winton touring car owned by A. B. Wharton, new husband of Tom Waggoner's daughter, Electra, and proprietor of the first auto dealership in Fort Worth. All 15 proud owners gathered near the Al Hayne monument in the T&P Plaza for a portrait.

The Boston investors who chartered the Northern Texas Traction Company in 1901 saw the great potential sparked by the growth of Fort Worth and Dallas. In 1902, the company inaugurated interurban service connecting the two cities. To power the electric streetcar line, NTTC built a new generating plant in the small town of Handley, six miles east of Fort Worth. The Interurban served the region until 1938, when the rail system gave way to buses. A restored car, similar to the ones photographed here in 1904, is on display at the Intermodal Transportation Center in downtown Fort Worth.

When Sam Rosen began to develop land near the growing stockyards in 1901, he assumed he would be able to work a deal with the Northern Texas Traction Company to provide rail access to his property. When NTTC declined, Rosen built his own line, running from the T&P station, across a new bridge over the river and out to North Fort Worth. The line required the construction of a crossing of the NTTC tracks that Rosen ingeniously accomplished in one night during a snowstorm in 1905, surprising his competitor the next morning and ensuring the success of Rosen Heights.

When storm damage in early 1908 closed the 1883 Opera House at Third and Rusk (now Commerce), theater manager Phil Greenwall worked with local developer A. T. Byers to build a larger Opera House at 7th and Rusk. Designed by Sanguinet and Staats, the new facility opened for the fall season and quickly became one of the premier performance venues in the region. By 1919, the name had changed to the Palace and movies replaced live productions. The building was demolished in 1977.

Fort Worth's City Park was laid out in 1892 along the stretch of the Trinity River between today's 7th Street and Lancaster Avenue bridges on the west side of Downtown. This image, from about 1905, views the park dam from a small bridge that crossed the river. Long a favorite spot for picnics and fishing, the dam and park were removed in the 1930s when the river channel was straightened and the Lancaster Bridge was built over the site.

The Improved Order of Red Men established chapters, or tribes, across the country throughout the nineteenth century. In 1907, its Fort Worth members gathered in full regalia around the Hayne Monument near the T&P Station. The organization's roots date to secret societies established prior to the American Revolution, including the Sons Of Liberty who poured British tea into Boston harbor. It continues its promotion of Freedom, Friendship, and Charity today.

A year after the 1898 fire that destroyed the Hurley Building at 7th and Main, Chicago businessman John R. Hoxie constructed a new building on the important corner. Among the building's early tenants was the law firm of Harris and Harris. Brothers W. D. and M. B. Harris both served as Tarrant County Judge, and W. D., elected mayor of Fort Worth in 1906, served during the South Side fire in 1909. The Hoxie Building's primary tenant, the Farmers and Mechanics Bank, acquired the property and demolished the building in 1920 to build a 24 story Sanguinet and Staats-designed skyscraper, then the tallest structure in the Southwest.

On 7th Street, at the intersection with Taylor, the local congregation of the Methodist Episcopal Church, South, built a new sanctuary in 1908, having outgrown their old home at 4th and Jones. The new building would serve the First Methodist Church until it built a newer sanctuary on 5th Street in 1931. Behind the fence at left was the full block of the A. J. Roe Lumber Yard, in operation since 1886. The yard site would become the home of the Fort Worth Club in 1926.

Fire fighters from Station Number One at Rusk (now Commerce) and 2nd streets proudly show off their new wagon and matched team of horses about 1905. The department vehicles got their unique white and gold colors when the men paid to have their entry in the annual State Fair pumper races painted by local buggy shop owner E. E. Lennox, who must have had more white paint on hand than red. The new colors were a hit, and remain part of the city's modern fleet.

Among the many buildings erected by the Stockyards Company was the 1908 Coliseum, shown here a year or so after construction. A group of dignitaries, perhaps in town for the activities of the annual Feeders and Breeders Show, stopped for the photographer. The Coliseum, completed in less than 90 working days and just in time for the 1908 show, has hosted a wide variety of events over the years, from a performance by Enrico Caruso to the modern weekly reenactments of traditional wild west shows.

Colonel Thomas M. Thannisch purchased the lot on the northeast corner of North Main and Exchange in 1904 as the Fort Worth Stockyards boomed following the arrival of the Swift and Armour companies. He built his Stock Yards Club Saloon and Billiards Parlor in 1906 and an adjoining brick hotel building in 1907. He later demolished the old club and built a bigger hotel that stands today as the Stockyards Hotel, welcoming visitors to the popular National Historic District.

The new seven-story Flatiron Building stands tall at far-left, looking north on Houston from 10th Street about 1907. The Lyric Theatre, at 1010 Houston opened that same year and presented vaudeville performances for 10 cents a ticket. In this view, telephone and electric wires create a conspicuous web over the city streets.

The photographer of the facing view of Houston Street turned his camera for a rare glimpse of 10th Street looking east. The smokestack belonged to the Texas Brewing Company. Its sprawling plant was built in 1890 along Jones, between 9th and 12th streets. This view would change dramatically after 1910 when the new Majestic Theatre opened on the Commerce Street site of the Darnell Lumber Company. The Majestic's owners lined 10th Street with white lights leading to the theater's front door, creating Fort Worth's own "Great White Way."

In 1908, the 1889 Board of Trade Building at the northwest corner of 7th and Houston remained one of the city's more elegant structures. The visions for the future that city promoters had touted from the rooftop observation deck had largely come true as Fort Worth was booming from the economic benefits of the stockyards and related businesses. The Continental Bank and Trust Company evolved into Continental National Bank, which demolished the old building in 1949 to make way for a new home for the bank.

St. Patrick Cathedral, left, completed in 1892, anchored a row of limestone buildings along Throckmorton, shown here looking north from 10th Street. Beyond the church are the 1893 city hall and the 1899 Central Fire Station. At right is the two-story Fort Worth Telephone Company building. Chartered in 1903, the phone company had about a thousand subscribers but could not successfully compete with the larger Southwestern Bell, which acquired the local company and its building in 1916.

The old and new worked side by side in 1910 as fire horses and a new fire truck posed at the 1899 Central Fire Station on Throckmorton Street. If no fire had been called in by 4:00 A.M. each day, the horses had to be exercised, and were usually ridden around the station. If the bell rang during this morning routine, an unwary fire fighter might well find himself swept off the horse as it raced back to the station and its place in the traces.

Founded in 1855, the First Christian Church congregation is the oldest in Fort Worth. Conducting their early services in a log house that had been part of the 1849 fort and then in the Masonic Lodge, the members built a frame church at Main and 4th Street about 1858. In 1878, under the leadership of Major K. M. Van Zandt, the congregation moved again, this time into its new stone sanctuary on Throckmorton, between 5th and 6th streets. Major Van Zandt would lead the church as Chairman of the Board until his death in 1930.

Having grown from about a dozen members to become one of the largest Disciples of Christ congregations in the world, First Christian hired architects Van Slyke and Woodruff to design a new sanctuary to replace the aging facility built in 1878. The new church was completed on the Throckmorton site in 1915. Adjacent to the church, on the right, was the 1,800 seat Chamber of Commerce Auditorium, opened in 1914.

The new miracle of electricity came to Fort Worth in 1885, providing a light on the courthouse tower and scattered streetlights downtown. By the time the North Main Street generating plant opened in 1912, most businesses and a few families had access to power. One of the first to offer modern lights and fixtures was the Bound Electric Company at 1006 Houston Street, just south of the Flatiron Building. The store's showroom seen here appears filled to capacity with choices of every shape, style and size.

In 1910, the Fort Worth Lodge number 124 of the Benevolent and Protective Order of Elks built a magnificent new clubhouse on the northwest corner of 7th and Lamar streets. Architecturally compatible with the neighboring homes of some of the city's wealthiest families, the lodge building served the club until 1928 when the Elks built a new facility at 4th and Lamar. The old clubhouse shown here was demolished about 1934.

The Fort Worth Fire Department purchased its first motorized vehicle in 1910. That year, the crew of Engine Company No. 5 proudly posed with the new equipment in front of their equally new station near South Main Street. The new firehouse replaced the nearby 1890 W. B. Tucker Hose Company No. 5.

At the busy intersection of 7th and Main, horse-drawn vehicles, automobiles, streetcars, pushcarts, and pedestrians compete for space about 1910. The 1899 Farmers and Mechanics Bank Building, formerly the Hoxie Building, stands at right. Immediately behind it to the west is the newly completed First National Bank Building facing its neighbor across Houston Street, the 1889 Board of Trade Building. At the far end of the view is the steeple of St. Paul's Methodist Episcopal Church. Of all the structures in this image, only the First National Building remains.

INTO THE MODERN ERA

(1911–1940)

A new First Baptist Church sanctuary nears completion on the southeast corner of Taylor and 4th streets in 1912. The church's 1886 building a block north on 3rd was destroyed by fire. Its charismatic but controversial young minister, J. Frank Norris, was accused and acquitted of arson. Norris led the church from 1909 until his death in 1952. In his early years, he compared Fort Worth to a modern Sodom and launched campaigns to clean up vice and corruption.

The courthouse and old jail dominate the skyline in this view looking up North Main. This photograph was taken about 1912, just after the Fort Worth Power and Light Company began operations of its coal-fired electricity generation plant.

The banner across Main Street dates this photograph to 1911 when a new Majestic Theatre opened on Commerce at 10th, replacing the smaller "old" Majestic built in 1905 on Jennings Avenue. The Majestic ushered in a new era of entertainment for the city, as leading performers and traveling road companies took advantage of the opulent facility. It was demolished in 1966.

Thirsty horses stop for a drink from the fountain in Peter Smith Park, just north of St. Patrick Cathedral between Jennings and Throckmorton. The small, triangular park was dedicated to Fort Worth pioneer John Peter Smith, called "the father of Fort Worth," shortly after his untimely death in 1901. He arrived in the young city in 1853, taught school, surveyed, practiced law, and, while serving as mayor from 1882 to 1885, oversaw big improvements in water supplies, street paving, and sanitation that moved Fort Worth into the modern age. He died following a robbery and assault while on a trip to promote the city.

On the opposite side of St. Patrick's Cathedral stands the 1888 St. Ignatius Academy, chartered in 1885 and operated by the Sisters of St. Mary of Namur. Architect J. J. Kane, who also designed the cathedral, designed the original academy building, at right. To accommodate the growing student body, the Sisters built an adjacent classroom building in 1905 that allowed the school to teach more than 400 students, many of them seen here filling the grounds and balconies. The 1905 structure was demolished in 1926 to make way for street expansion.

Risking the windy conditions, pioneering French pilot Roland Garros, standing in the middle with moustache, completed the first flight in Fort Worth on January 12, 1911, in his Bleriot monoplane. Thrilling a crowd of more than 15 thousand spectators gathered at the Driving Park on 7th Street, Garros and other pilots of International Aviators spent two days of a national tour igniting Fort Worth's passion for aviation. Garros died in 1918 when his plane was shot down during World War I.

NAT. FEEDERS & BREEDERS SHOW 1916
FAMOUS "6666"
GRAND CHAMPIONS.
RAISED BY S.B.BURNETT.   FED BY SID WILLIAMS.
BOUGHT BY SWIFT & COMPANY.
12 cts. HIGHEST PRICE CATTLE U.S.1916.

Key to the successful marketing of the Fort Worth facilities was the Annual Feeders and Breeders Show, forerunner of today's Southwestern Exposition and Livestock Show. Tracing its roots to 1896, the show rapidly developed a reputation of introducing some of the finest livestock in the country. In 1916, Captain S. B. Burnett proudly displayed the Grand Champions from his Four Sixes Ranch, the products of careful breeding to enhance the quality of beef available to American consumers.

By World War I, the Stockyards had grown into the largest horse and mule market in the world, and competed for the third-largest in terms of general livestock activity in the United States. Here, the Swift & Company plant, with its columned 1902 headquarters building, rises above Exchange Avenue and rail spurs packed with freight cars.

Young women of the Fort Worth Colored High School stood for their group portrait in front of the school in 1918. Three years later, the segregated campus would be renamed for education pioneer Isaiah M. Terrell. Arriving in Fort Worth in 1882, Terrell headed the first public school established in the city for African-Americans. By the time he left in 1915 to head what would become Prairie View A&M University, Terrell had established a tradition of teaching and academic excellence that continued for decades under such noted educators as Dr. Hazel Harvey Peace.

Following a merger of his Waggoner Bank & Trust with First National Bank in 1917, cattle and oil man W. T. Waggoner demolished his old bank building at 8th and Houston and hired Sanguinet and Staats to design the tallest building in Fort Worth as a replacement. Waggoner got the better of friend and fellow cattleman S. B. Burnett, who owned what was then the current tallest structure, the 13-story Burk Burnett Building. Waggoner proudly dedicated his 20-story skyscraper in 1919.

The view south on Main Street from 3rd about 1921 presented an interesting mix of old and new buildings. Beyond the nineteenth-century row at left, the just-finished Farmers and Mechanics Bank rises at 7th Street. At 24 stories, it was the tallest building in the Southwest. The 7-story Westbrook Hotel stands at right, with the Burk Burnett Building just beyond.

The view of Houston Street looking south from 3rd about 1921 illustrates the tremendous growth around the midtown financial and business center, which was expanding on either side of the 7th Street corridor. The Farmers and Mechanics Bank tower rises at left, with the W. T. Waggoner Building on the west side of the street at 8th. Uptown, closer to the courthouse, remnants of the city's nineteenth-century architecture still dominate the streetscape.

Starting in Dallas in 1901, Fishburn's Steam Laundry expanded to Fort Worth in 1909, opening at 501 Rusk Street, soon to be renamed Commerce Street. Having graduated from horse-drawn delivery wagons, Fishburn's promoted its new automobile delivery with "Service Always in the Lead." The monumental lettering on the building, coupled with internally lighted orbs spelling the company name, extending over the street from the pole at right, allowed the newly established business to promote itself day and night.

When America entered World War I, Fort Worth rallied to the cause. It was selected in 1917 as the home of Camp Bowie, a sprawling military base built on the city's west side to house and train 100,000 Texas and Oklahoma National Guard soldiers for the 36th Division. Before departing for the war in Europe, the troops staged a massive "Pass in Review" on April 11, 1918. Here, soldiers march up Main Street cheered by a crowd that local accounts say reached 200,000. The 36th became known as the Panther Division, adopted from Fort Worth's nickname, Panther City.

Before Camp Bowie officially closed after World War I, Fort Worth hosted another parade for the troops stationed there. Marching south on lower Main Street in June 1919, the Camp Bowie Band leads the column. The street and other infrastructure improvements made by the Army for the camp served to jump-start development of the west side following the war.

Fort Worth's first Park Board convened in 1907, but struggled for adequate funding during its early years. The local Rotary Club, under the leadership of one of its founders, Harry Adams, raised money to pay for park acquisition and support the development of the Park Department, including purchasing equipment like a new International truck.

The view north on Main Street from 11th in 1921 illustrates the changing times for local theaters. While the Majestic advertises its vaudeville fair with a huge banner across the street, the Hippodrome, at left, features a first-run silent movie melodrama, *Playthings of Destiny*. A decade later, the Majestic itself would be converted to a movie house and end live performances.

At the time the staff of the Fort Worth *Star-Telegram* sat for this photograph about 1920, the paper served more than 80 Texas counties and proudly boasted on its masthead, "Fort Worth—Where the West Begins." Owner and Publisher Amon G. Carter was one of the most influential local leaders of the twentieth century, promoting his city and all of West Texas to the world.

To meet the growing demands for space in the Stockyards following the opening of Swift and Armour, Colonel C. M. Thannisch demolished his Stock Yards Club hotel and office building at North Main and Exchange in 1906 and built the Thannisch Block. It featured expanded lodging rooms and space for new businesses, including the Exchange Drug Store. By the twenties, the building housed the 86-room Chandler Hotel.

The intersection of 7th and Lamar streets about 1915 marked a neighborhood in transition, as what had been the silk-stocking neighborhood began a shift from residential to commercial use. It was home to some of the city's wealthiest families, including that of Winfield Scott, who owned several of the largest hotels and other buildings in the city. At right is the 1890 sanctuary of the Saint Paul Methodist Episcopal Church, replaced in 1929 by the Electric Building. The 1910 clubhouse of the Fort Worth Elks Lodge stands at left. Between them hangs one of the city's early electric street lights.

Eager customers crowded the front door of the new Montgomery Ward store on West 7th Street on its first day of business in 1928. In the background, at top-right, is the massive assembly plant built and used by Chevrolet from 1915 to 1922, and which Wards occupied until it moved into its new building across the street. Left of the assembly plant was the towering elevator complex of the E. G. Rall Grain Company, built in 1913. Both complexes were demolished in the 1980s.

Montgomery Ward stock boys were issued roller skates to maneuver around the eight-story, 300,000-square-foot warehouse in order to meet demands of its mail-order department. The store closed in 2001, reemerging in 2006 as Montgomery Plaza, a mixed-use development with loft apartments.

Margarito Padilla left his native San Luis Potosi, Mexico, to escape the dangers of the revolution that began there in 1910. He found work at Swift & Company in the Stockyards, then the city's largest employer, where he remained until he retired in the 1960s. On November 28, 1926, he married Maria P. Felan, daughter of a South Texas family, at the old San Jose Church on North Calhoun Street. Together they raised a family that continues to help shape the future of the city.

This aerial view of downtown, taken October 6, 1926, shows the Medical Arts Building still under construction at lower-left, with residential neighborhoods to its south and west. Just above Burnett Park stands the Elks Lodge and, to its right, the empty lot on which the Electric Building would be built in 1930.

Taken in Burnett Park sometime in the mid-twenties, this photograph by Roy Jernigan is believed to show a group of relatives of Comanche chief Quanah Parker. They may have been in town to participate in the annual Stock Show Parade. Before Parker's death in 1911, he had been a frequent visitor to Fort Worth. His descendants continue their active involvement in city activities. The Elks Club building, at top-right, stood on the corner of Lamar and 7th streets.

Starting in the late twenties, Fort Worth began a massive street improvement program, working with the T&P Railroad to improve rail crossings at the south end of Downtown before turning attention to other areas. By January 1934, construction was well under way on a new overpass on Belknap Street, east of Downtown, allowing motorists to safely drive over the ever-expanding rail tracks surrounding the city.

The highlight of 1936 in Fort Worth was the opening of the Casa Manana amphitheater, the star of the Frontier Centennial celebrating Texas's 100th anniversary of independence from Mexico. Through one of the hottest summers on record, people crowded the 4,000-seat open-air theater to enjoy the music of Paul Whiteman and watch a spectacular show produced by Broadway's Billy Rose.

The annual Stock Show parade took on a patriotic theme for the Texas Centennial year and celebrated "the Spirit of the Old West." A few antique automobiles and stilt walkers joined the usual bands and mounted groups on a sunny and warm parade day on March 13, 1936. The year marked the Fort Worth show's recognition by *Time* magazine as the "number three" rodeo in the nation.

Pedestrians cross the intersection of 7th and Throckmorton streets in 1938. Headlining at the Worth Theatre is Dave Apollon, considered the greatest mandolin player of the twentieth century. He toured the country regularly, including several stops in Fort Worth before settling down to a recording and theatrical career in New York.

A column marches past the Sinclair Building during the annual Armistice Day Parade on November 11, 1936. Commemorating the cease-fire that marked the end of World War I, the holiday was an important one for Fort Worth, which had supported so many young men as they trained at Camp Bowie between 1917 and 1919.

The Jennings Avenue viaduct provides a commanding view looking north toward the Carnegie Library in 1931. The next year, the viaduct was demolished and replaced with an underpass as part of the street and rail-crossing improvements jointly undertaken by the city and the T&P Railroad. The city was so grateful for the railroad's financial partnership that Front Street was renamed in honor of John L. Lancaster, the company president at the time.

The same view from the Jennings viaduct as the preceding page, but taken more than 25 years earlier, before the perfection of elevators allowed for the construction of high-rise buildings. The distinctive 1889 St. Ignatius Academy, and behind it St. Patrick Cathedral, remain today as benchmarks of the city's growth and progress over the years.

An aerial photographer captured Arlington Downs on a crowded race day in October 1933. Over 27,000 spectators gathered at the track, which was built by Fort Worth cattle and oil baron W. T. Waggoner 16 miles east of the city to showcase his family's championship horse-breeding program. Considered the finest private racing facility in the nation when it opened in 1929, the track closed in 1937 after gambling opponents forced the repeal of pari-mutuel betting in Texas.

During the Great Depression, Fort Worth benefited from the power wielded in Washington by a strong Texas delegation that included local Congressman Fritz G. Lanham. With the aid of tax-generated federal funds in 1938, the city built a new city hall on the site of the old 1893 municipal building. To the right of the new hall in this photograph, taken in February 1939, is the 1899 Central Fire Station and the foundation for the new public library on the site of the old Carnegie Library. At far-left is the turreted corner of the nineteenth-century Federal Building.

Proprietor Charles Reichenstein moved his Worth Segar Store into the prestigious Worth Building at 7th and Main in 1932. Son of a German immigrant to Texas, the football standout from Texas A&M moved to Fort Worth about 1912. While building his businesses, he launched a nearly 20-year career as a high school and college football referee, retiring in 1933 as the acknowledged dean of the profession. His store was the city's center for sports scores, tickets, and storytelling until the depression-era economy forced it to close in 1938. "Charlie Rick" continued to operate his other store in the Livestock Exchange Building until his death in 1949.

Among the many public improvements funded by city bonds and federal grants during the depression was a massive street repaving program. During the spring and summer of 1938, downtown streets were recovered with hundreds of thousands of bricks, laid atop sand and asphalt. In this image by the talented amateur photographer Lewis Fox, pedestrians have stopped to watch the professional bricklayers create a perfect street surface in the 700 block of Main Street.

The view west on 7th Street from Summit Avenue about 1936 shows Fort Worth's "Automobile Row," where most of the city's dealerships and shops operated. The recently completed First Methodist Church commands the skyline at left while the Neil P. Anderson Building, center at the head of the street, welcomes visitors to downtown.

A January 1940 snowfall highlights the fairgrounds built for the Texas Centennial in 1936, and the area that would evolve into Fort Worth's Cultural District. Having seen its last season in 1939, the remarkable 4,000-seat Casa Mañana amphitheater, at center, would be demolished in 1942.

From its very first year in 1896, the annual Stock Show has kicked off with a parade. At first, a few businesses decorated floats and wagons to accompany the working cowboys in a simple procession along North Main Street. Eventually, the parade moved Downtown and evolved into one of the longest non-mechanized annual processions in the world. Here, two riders move down Main Street for the opening of the 1938 show.

MIDCENTURY CHANGES

(1941–1960s)

During a national War Bond tour in 1943, the Japanese "midget sub" captured at Pearl Harbor in December 1941 made its way to Fort Worth. Displayed near the intersection of Houston and 9th streets, the sub attracted enthusiastic crowds during its short stay. The vessel now resides within the Pacific War artifacts collection of the National Museum of the Pacific War, formerly the Admiral Nimitz Museum, in Fredericksburg, Texas.

A light dusting of snow invited a photographer to venture out to capture Houston Street looking south from 6th. The ornate nineteenth-century Board of Trade Building would shortly disappear from its place on 7th Street, but the W. T. Waggoner Building in the next block and the Flatiron farther down the street would remain.

Pedestrians dodging mounds of snow piled high in the center of Houston Street between 4th and 5th had plenty of opportunities to escape the cold in this heart of the Downtown shopping district where local retailers far outnumbered national and regional chains.

On April 9, 1942, just three weeks after the 1942 Stock Show closed, another of Fort Worth's devastating floods damaged so much of the property in the Stockyards that the show was canceled for 1943. Wartime priorities hampered the show's regrouping, but when the exposition was fully up and running again in 1946, it had made a permanent move to the West Side and the Will Rogers Complex.

A crowd of evacuated moviegoers block 7th Street while emergency teams check the Worth Theater for any damage. The Robert Young and Laraine Day film playing that afternoon was a light comedy that opened in June 1945, just a month after Victory in Europe (VE) Day. With the nation still fighting in the Pacific, it's a safe bet that most of the young men in uniform would have preferred a cozy, dark theater to the excitement captured in this photograph.

The 1893 Al Hayne Monument, center, presides over the much-changed intersection of Main and Lancaster in the 1940s. At far-right, the Frank Kent Ford dealership occupies the site of the former T&P Passenger Station. Just below the horizon at right is the I. M. Terrell High School, completed in 1937 and named for the distinguished educator who came to Fort Worth in 1882 as head of the first school for African-Americans in the city.

Army vehicles move north on Main Street during a parade to honor Jonathan Wainwright, the highest-ranking American taken prisoner in World War II. Temporarily promoted to lieutenant general on Corregidor, the Philippines, he was forced to surrender his troops to the Japanese in 1942. After three years as a POW, he was present for the Japanese surrender aboard the USS *Missouri* in 1945 and returned to a hero's welcome in the United States.

Long before the construction of branch libraries during the sixties, the Fort Worth Public Library toured neighborhoods and schools, attracting young readers with its Bookmobile. The traveling library service began in 1948 under the auspices of Library director Joseph Ibbotson, who also started the Friends of the Library organization.

The two-story Dundee Building, built before 1898 on the southeast corner of 7th and Houston streets. Its tenants included the flagship store of Fort Worth's 13 Renfro Drug Stores and the studios of pioneering photographers Charles Swartz and Roy Jernigan. The Fort Worth National Bank demolished the building in 1950 to erect a new skyscraper on the site.

The Flood of May 1949 brought water close to the intersection of West 7th and Arch Adams streets, allowing dockside service to both the Seventh Street Theatre and the renowned Kleinschmidt's Bake Shop. In the distance are Montgomery Ward's and the tower of the Medical Arts Building.

By the time of the May 1949 flood, the Fort Worth Stockyards had already started on the slow decline to closure after the peak year of 1944, when 5.25 million animals were processed through the packing and rail facilities. Armour and Company closed in 1962, followed by Swift's in 1971. The sprawling plants shown here have largely disappeared, with the exception of the columned Swift headquarters, center, restored in 2007. The hog and sheep pens, at left, were converted to the modern Stockyards Station, a leading attraction in the National Historic District created in 1976 through the efforts of the North Fort Worth Historical Society, a volunteer organization whose museum in the District is dedicated to preserving the remarkable legacy of the livestock industry in Fort Worth.

Across town, journalism students at Texas Christian University in 1949 established the whimsical TCU Yacht Club, commanding the waters of the fish pond in front of the Mary Couts Burnett Library. Among the "Admirals" of the club was Jack White, fourth from left, who went on to a long public relations career in Fort Worth and whose efforts to preserve the photographic history of the city helped protect for the future many of the images included in this book.

In commemoration of the 100th anniversary of the founding of Fort Worth, local riders reenacted the June 6, 1849, arrival of the Second United States Dragoons on the bluff overlooking the confluence of the Clear and West forks of the Trinity River. Fort founder Major Ripley A. Arnold was portrayed by local celebrity Walker Moore as the soldiers paraded up Main Street and passed in front of the courthouse, built near the site of the original military camp.

A crowd gathers to watch Fort Worth fire fighters battle a blaze on the south end of Downtown about 1950. By that time, many of the old buildings in the once-vibrant business section had fallen into disrepair or were used for inexpensive housing—"flop houses," as one veteran fire fighter recalled. Much of this area would be demolished a decade later to make way for the Convention Center.

Fire Prevention Week was ably promoted throughout the sixties by the Fire Department's Miss Flame, whose duties included public appearances and parades. Behind her is one of Fort Worth's oldest stores, tracing its roots to 1889 when William Monnig arrived in Fort Worth to open a dry goods store. As owner of "the Friendly Store," Monnig served many leadership roles in the city, including heading up the Frontier Centennial Committee in 1936. In 1990, the company he founded was the last of the downtown retailers to move to the suburbs.

Fort Worth's oldest African-American congregation was organized in 1866 and formally chartered in 1868 as Morning Chapel Colored Methodist Episcopal Church. In 1885, the church housed the first high school for African-American students in the area, a program that evolved into the venerable I. M. Terrell High School that educated generations of community leaders. Nearly a century after the church's founding, members of the senior choir and their director, Mrs. Norvelle Stewart, far right, pose for a portrait by noted local photographer Calvin Littlejohn.

The new First National Bank Building, center, built in 1961 and designed by Skidmore, Owings and Merrill, introduced modern architecture to Fort Worth. This view, looking east on 10th Street from Henderson toward the Medical Arts Building and Federal Courthouse, shows the heart of the Automobile Row dealerships that extended along 7th Street. Texas Motors Ford started at this location in 1943.

When construction began on Midway Airport in 1950, the new airfield was heralded as the long sought solution to settling the dispute between Fort Worth and Dallas over which city would dominate air services in the region. Dallas leaders balked because the airport lobby faced west to Fort Worth, and they refocused their energies to expand Love Field. The new airport built midway between the two cities was then renamed Greater Fort Worth International Airport. The two rivals eventually worked together to open Dallas Fort Worth International Airport in 1974, necessitating the closure of Amon Carter Field, as the midway facility had come to be called.

On November 21, 1963, President and Mrs. John F. Kennedy arrived in Fort Worth during a swing through Texas to rally Democratic leaders in advance of the 1964 elections. The Kennedys stayed the night at the Texas Hotel and attended a breakfast hosted by the chamber of commerce the next morning, before traveling to Dallas for a planned speech there. As he departed, the president greeted some of the sheriff's department mounted officers assigned to secure the area.

The president made a few remarks to a crowd of about 8,000 gathered outside the hotel on the drizzly morning of the 22nd and casually greeted some of the crowd before moving inside to the more formal chamber of commerce breakfast. Before heading to Carswell Air Force Base in a convertible borrowed from Ben Hogan, the Kennedys had an opportunity to enjoy a special art exhibit created for their hotel suite that included works borrowed from some of the museums and private collections in town. In Dallas later that day, Kennedy would be assassinated.

By 1950, few new buildings had been added to the city's skyline since the boom building years of the 1920s. The 1896 Federal Building can be seen at bottom center, and the tallest structure in town was still the 1921 Fort Worth National Bank Building at 7th and Main. Great changes were on the horizon as Fort Worth struggled with one of the pressing urban issues of the day—how to keep Downtown alive as suburban growth skyrocketed.

Drivers entering Downtown from the Jacksboro Highway across the Henderson Street Bridge were greeted for years by the elegant character on a liquor billboard, a not-altogether-unfitting reminder of the roadway's wild past. The 1957 Continental National Bank Building, with its enormous revolving clock dominates the skyline about 1962, after the completion of a new

The face of Downtown began to change dramatically during the 1950s as once-bustling commercial areas and expensive residential neighborhoods began to fall to the wrecking ball under federal programs like Urban Renewal rather than being renovated. In 1966, the demolition of the magnificent 1910 Majestic Theatre at 10th and Commerce led to the removal of 13 blocks of buildings along Main Street below 9th for the construction of the Tarrant County Convention Center, completed in 1968. The merits of historic preservation would not rise to the forefront of national consciousness until the 1970s, after the destruction of many buildings worth saving in cities like Fort Worth.

Built about 1889 as the first house in the new Arlington Heights subdivision, this classical Victorian home was probably constructed for the development's first president, George Tallant. Considered one of a dozen most important buildings worthy of preservation in Fort Worth in a 1969 study commissioned by Historic Fort Worth, the house was nevertheless demolished to make way for new development in 1970. Robert McCart, an early Fort Worth business leader who provided financial backing for the Texas Spring Palace and gave land for the development of Camp Bowie during World War I, owned the house for many years.

Fort Worth *Press* and later *Star-Telegram* photographer Gene Gordon captured this group of serious future fire fighters during a "Sparky Party" at Station 26 at Hulen and Trail Lake in the early 1960s. Thousands of Fort Worth children learned fire safety from Captain William "Fireman Bill" Pierce, who, with Captain Luther Koch, created an innovative teaching tool, the "Sparky Fire Department," in 1954.

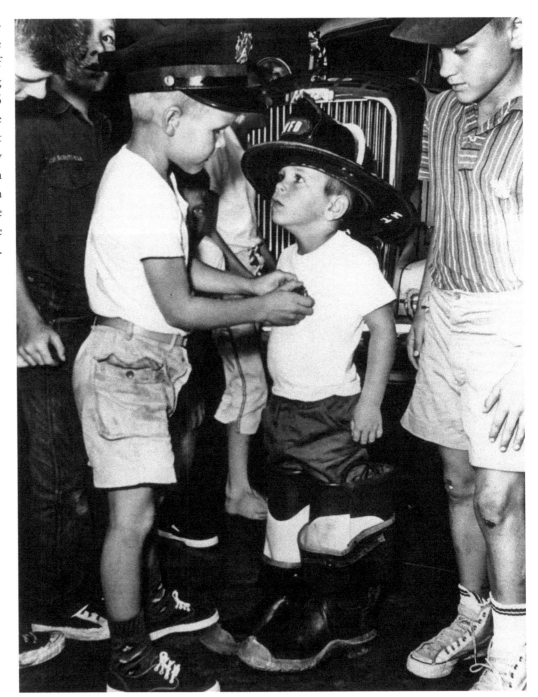

During a routine scuba training dive at Lake Benbrook in the late 1960s, members of the rescue team found a submerged 1947 Studebaker, verified by the police as having been stolen many years earlier. As the recovered car drained on shore, surprised fire fighters heard something move in the trunk. This photograph of the 67- and 68-pound catfish that had evidently grown up in the back of the car hit the wire services and ran worldwide.

In this photo taken about 1968, the Flatiron Building's former neighbors, the Lyric Theatre and Robertson's Funeral Home, have been replaced with a hotel and the Southwestern Bell Building beyond it. Long considered one of Fort Worth's most important and beloved structures, the Flatiron enters its second century completely restored, a reminder of the early dreams of its builders.

Notes on the Photographs

These notes, listed by page number, attempt to include all aspects known of the photographs. Each of the photographs is identified by the page number, a title or description, photographer and collection, archive, and call or box number when applicable. Although every attempt was made to collect all data, in some cases complete data may have been unavailable due to the age and condition of some of the photographs and records.

Printed in the USA
CPSIA information can be obtained
at www.ICGtesting.com
JSHW072024140824
68134JS00042B/3772